INTENTIONAL LIVING

SIMON GORDON

INTENTIONAL LIVING
© Copyright 2011
by Simon Gordon

Unless otherwise noted, all Scripture quotations are taken from the Holy Bible, King James Version.

Scripture quotations marked NKJV are from the Holy Bible, New King James Version. Copyright © 1982, Thomas Nelson, Inc. Used by permission.

Scripture quotations marked NIV are from the Holy Bible, New International Version. Copyright © 1973, 1978, 1984, International Bible Society. Used by Permission.

All rights reserved. This book is protected under the copyright laws of the United States of America. This book may not be copied or reprinted for commercial gain or profit. The use of short quotations or occasional page copying for personal or group study is permitted and encouraged. Permission will be granted upon request.

ISBN: 978-0-9845874-1-4

Published by

LIFEBRIDGE
BOOKS
P.O. BOX 49428
CHARLOTTE, NC 28277

Printed in the United States of America.

Dedication

It is with great joy that I dedicate this book to my father, the late Rev. Joseph P. Gordon and my mother, the late Lady Lessie Gordon. They were the epitome of great parentage with the wisdom, love, discipline and order they displayed as a lifestyle before me. I will always miss them. Both of my parents were educators and took much pleasure in teaching hundreds of people the value of loving to learn.

Dad as a professor in various seminaries and mom as a piano and elementary teacher shaped the lives of parishioners and their children.

They clearly taught the value of character and integrity and demonstrated this nugget of continual wisdom:

Never conclude a matter until you have exhausted all of its contradictions.

Psalmist wisdom is parallel to the wisdom they shared with all, and my desire is to have my mission statement fulfilled in life toward humanity:

*To please God with every aspect of my life,
To positively influence all I come in contact with,
To empower and impact others toward pursuit of
destiny and godly living, To leave a legacy for
my children and teach them to do the same
for the generation following.*

Contents

	Introduction	7
1	Something Marvelous is Happening in You!	11
2	The Power of Passion	29
3	Time to Join the "Happy People"	51
4	Improved, Impressive, and Magnificently Designed	69
5	Celebrate Greatness and Pass it On!	87
6	Get Ready to Take Off!	99
7	They Prayed, They Praised, and Then They Danced!	109
8	"I'm Going to Live Intentionally"	125

INTRODUCTION

The fact that you have chosen to read this book tells me something important. You are not content with the status quo and want more out of life. You don't want to succeed by accident or happenstance—but intentionally.

In my lifelong study of God's Word, I have found that one book stands above the rest when it comes to giving counsel, wisdom, and direction for living. It is the book of Psalms.

In these pages I want you to discover the heart of David as he tells us what is truly essential in life. As a result, I believe you will take an introspective look at yourself to see how you measure up—emotionally, relationally, and spiritually.

I hesitate to deal with negatives, but let's begin by defining what having a full life *is* and is *not*. It is not:

- Having unlimited earthly possessions.
- Having many positive and negative experiences.
- Having tried everything under the sun.

A full life is to know and enjoy an intimate relationship with and in God!

If you aren't careful, life's challenges will teach you how to be no more than a professional underachiever. To put it another way, if you are not living intentionally you are probably living accidentally!

Now that I know better, I want the world to understand where my help comes from. As the psalmist tells us, *"My flesh and my heart faileth: but God is the strength [rock] of my heart, and my portion for ever"* (Psalm 73:26).

In this book you will learn:

- The key to seeing something marvelous happen in you.
- The purpose and power of passion.
- How to join the "Happy People."
- You are improved, impressive, and magnificently designed.
- Why you should celebrate greatness and pass it on.
- How to reach new spiritual heights.
- The secret of unlimited praise.
- How to put intentional living into practice.

Let me encourage you to read with an open heart. Allow the Lord to shine His loving searchlight into your very soul. If there are habits, emotions, or attitudes that need to be changed, the Lord will show you. Most important, when you practice daily the divine principles of praise as found in the psalms, your entire life will take on new meaning. God will reveal the vision, will, and purpose He has for you.

It is my prayer that as a result of reading this book, your future will come into sharper focus and you will be a walking testimony of *Intentional Living*.

– Simon Gordon

1

Something Marvelous is Happening in You!

Thou hast beset me behind and before, and laid thine hand upon me. Such knowledge is too wonderful for me; it is high, I cannot attain unto it....For thou hast possessed my reins: thou hast covered me in my mother's womb. I will praise thee; for I am fearfully (yare'=to be awed or awesome) and wonderfully (palah=distinct, distinguished, or set apart) made: marvellous are thy works; and that my soul knoweth, right well.

– Psalm 139:5-6, 13-14

I believe we are in the midst of a marvelous act of God. Why? Because so many things that are taking place among God's people have never occurred before. I see men and women desiring Him with greater intensity. They look at what is happening around them and don't want to be left out of what God is going to do next. This is why we must pray to our heavenly Father, "Include me, in what You are saying and doing."

If you are faithful to the Lord, Psalm 139 will encourage you on the journey. However, if you are attempting to hide from God, this psalm will make you realize you are fighting a losing battle. Wherever you go, the Lord is watching.

The reason this is such a powerful psalm is because it addresses not only the omnipotence of God but also His omniscience and omnipresence. It deals with the fact that the Almighty is everywhere at all times, He is all-powerful, and knows everything.

Because God changes not, there is nothing we can do to alter what He knows, who He is, what He does, or how He wants to accomplish His will.

This places us in a unique position, because if we

accept the truth of this passage, we will realize that our life is full of new and undiscovered benefits. Certain forces merge, evolve, and embrace our lives because they are shaped and formed to fit the framework of our future. The central issue is for us to truly know God and ourselves. The Creator has empowered us to be who we are regarding Him. However, it is vital that we resist the power of choice God has given us to misbehave and remain outside the vision He has for our tomorrow.

A Marvel of Divine Engineering

In Psalm 139:13, when David speaks of the amazing development of a baby in his mother's womb, the very thought is miraculous. Think of it! As author William McDonald wrote, "In a speck of watery material smaller than the dot over this i, all the future characteristics of the child are programmed—the color of his skin, eyes and hair, the shape of his facial features, the natural abilities he will have. All that the child will be physically and mentally is contained in germ form in that fertilized egg. From it will develop: 60 trillion cells, 100 thousand miles of nerve fiber, 60 thousand miles of vessels carrying blood around the body, 250 bones, to say nothing of joints, ligaments and muscles."

David describes this formation of the fetus with

exquisite delicacy and beauty. *"You formed my inward parts; You covered me in my mother's womb"* (Psalm 139:13 NKJV). Every fiber of our being is a marvel of divine engineering.

Consider the brain, for instance, with its capacity for recording facts, sounds, and sights—with its incredible ability to recall and make decisions. This was all knit together by God in our mother's womb.

YOU ARE A PROMISE

You are more than a unique creation. God made you for a purpose!

Far too many are living beneath their privilege. I hope you realize the potential we have because we belong to our heavenly Father. We must learn to trust where He is leading and walk boldly through doors He opens. When He is your guide, there will be moments when you exclaim, "Whoa! I wasn't expecting that."

The Lord wants to place something inside you that you can't fully understand, but He is waiting for you to allow Him to have full control. Let Him release amazing things in your life today.

Whether you recognize this or not, your future is full of promise and success.

What is a promise? It is a vow of guaranteed results

—a settled word. As the psalmist writes, *"For ever, O Lord, thy word is settled in heaven"* (Psalm 119:89). We must never forget that what God says is sealed and true.

Our obedience to His will determines our participation in His blessings.

If we go ahead and start doing what He has already shown us, we will begin to enjoy His favor. The blessing is not that we acquire "stuff" or are prosperous, it is so we can exemplify to others who God truly is. He wants the world to know that there is a wealth of wonder that dwells in the earth He created.

INVADE YOUR POTENTIAL

Each of us are placed on this planet to be a blessing. Think about what you had to overcome and conquer to be where you are today. Look at the obstacles you had to tunnel through.

Never excuse the fullness and righteousness God has placed within you—or whose Name you represent, making you who you are. When you claim your divine heritage and know your place in God's family, you will firmly stand in the authority and realm of righteousness.

Who you are will shout loud and clear and radiate brightly.

Ignore what the critics say and allow God to stand tall inside you.

The world may be filled with chaos, the government may be floundering, and the economy may be out of control, but remember that with the Lord you still have a great future ahead.

Start invading your potential and understand that you have more going for you than you realize. However the challenge of achieving your potential is threefold: (1) respect it, (2) recognize it, and (3) respond to it.

When you activate these three ingredients you place a demand on the promises that God has said belong to you. I am convinced that on this journey we have to make a spiritual demand on everything in the earth that is presently ours. This is how we see it manifested. We have to literally say to the Almighty, "God, You declared this in Your Word. You told me that if I obey You and walk in Your way, these things will come to pass. So I am waiting, Lord, for You to overtake these obstacles and give me victory."

Your Day of Triumph

When you walk in the light of righteousness, hidden opportunities are uncovered just by asking God to reveal them. The Lord has much in store, but you need to let Him know how deeply you want His favor. Pray, "Heavenly Father, show me what I have not seen. Do for me what has not been done. Give me what I have not experienced. Teach me how to express what I have been unable to say."

From the moment you wake up in the morning, be ready to receive. As a soldier on the battlefield, you can't be caught snoozing—waiting on the sidelines for someone to tell you it is time to fight for your future. Instead, you should be alert, proclaiming, "Whatever God has for me, I'm going after it."

Owning up to who God says you are in the earth is an awesome thing!

There should be at least one victory you win over the enemy every day. You shouldn't have to go to church to get the devil off your back. God has already cleaned the slate. For this reason, each day should be another 24 hours of triumph.

You Can't Surprise God

If we are to have integrity and honesty in our

relationship with God, we need more than fellowship, spirituality, and anointing. We also need consecration. It is essential that we go through the sanctification process—to be set aside for the Lord and dedicated to His eternal purpose.

As Psalm 139:5 tells us, *"Thou hast beset me behind and before, and laid thine hand upon me."*

Before you attempt to wander away from God or choose a path that detours you from His purpose, remember that He knows everything you do and think. The Lord sees whether you are uplifting His Name or letting Him down.

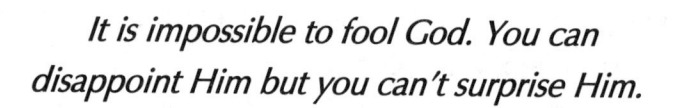

It is impossible to fool God. You can disappoint Him but you can't surprise Him.

At some point, it is our obligation to offer ourselves deliberately to Him. As the Apostle Paul counseled, *"I beseech you therefore, brethren, by the mercies of God, that ye present your bodies a living sacrifice, holy, acceptable unto God, which is your reasonable service"* (Romans 12:1).

When you do this, don't be surprised when the Lord starts offering your life to others.

He hears you when you say, "God, I'm open. I am

ready to be who You say I am." Stay undeniably connected and irreversibly attached!

Can the Lord offer you to those around you? Can He call your name as an example of how He blesses in the earth? Can He use you and your situations to show that you came from the gutter and went to the penthouse? I'm not talking about acting low, rather about living low—having to go through trials and coming out in grand fashion because of who God is in your life.

The moment you commit to changing your thinking and acting, He will release His favor. God will make you a target. I don't mean a bull's-eye for the enemy to attack, but a dynamo for the Lord to bless.

The good things that are taking place in your life today are only a foretaste of what He has planned.

THE GREAT MYSTERY

If you think all this sounds mysterious, it is. So don't treat your mystery like it is a problem. Your problems only have answers, but mysteries provide clues God uses to reveal His ultimate plan. You may not understand exactly how He is going to fit the pieces together, but He has the master plan.

So never get frustrated or upset with the trials and tribulations which are associated with fulfilling His purpose. Remember, it's not a problem, just a mystery. You may not like being pushed back, pressed down, and sometimes having to be patient and wait. But understand that in the process God is making you a better package He intends to deliver. He has to shape you to go places you could not fit before—for the future He has ordained.

Know that when God limits you it is not always a demotion; it is likely a promotion!

It's "Boundless"

Even the yoke of the Lord that is on your life reveals His care for you! When Jesus said, *"Take my yoke upon you"* (Matthew 11:29), the word *yoke* implies being tied up, restrained, limited, harnessed, able to control or keep in order. The yoke does not take away your liberty, it *defines* your liberty!

I discovered that until I was yoked with the Master I had not learned to properly practice my freedoms. After all, boundlessness and limitlessness combined with immaturity produces recklessness!

The purpose of the yoke is to cause us to lose our right to be reckless and get us centered on our real destiny!

As you uncover God's vision designed just for you, you'll shout "Praise the Lord!"

The benefit of praising God because you know who you are in Him makes you free to express the boundlessness of liberty:

- Boundless sharing produces innocent persuasion and unquestionable trust!
- Boundless praise produces innocent pursuance and unquestionable affection!
- Boundless worship produces innocent surrender and unquestionable faith!

A New You

Remember, God made you, planned your potential, and ordered your days.

This is not some kind of blind fatalism that paralyzes your every thought and move. It is the wise plan of a loving Father who knows what is best for His child.

———————⋙———————

Accept who you are as His gift to you, and then use it wisely as your gift to Him.

Take joy in the mystery. Let Him repackage your future and send you where He has destined.

Start rejoicing in what God is doing in your life. Driving your car or walking down the street, have conversations with Him and let Him know how wonderful He is. Even when there are past due bills mounting on the table, you can sing His praises because you are enjoying this blessed mystery. God is working things out for your good.

Why would the Lord give us mystery? Because it is only by faith that we learn to master our mysteries. He places us in a position that unless we operate in faith we are not going to receive answers to our prayers. For example, we cannot access the expressions of the Father unless we do so by spirit and faith. This being the case, the situations we endure are not hindrances.

Your troubles are not really your destiny, only your itinerary. They are just stops you are making on the way to God's eternal purpose for you.

The Lord established this process because His assignments are meant to challenge us. Be aware that when God begins to do a good work in you, He separates you from the pack—pulling you away from certain people. After all, they don't really understand who you are in Christ. The world starts judging your ability and even your support cast become spectators. You may even have more cheerleaders than individuals who can walk by your side.

THE WINGS OF MORNING

When God determines to use you, He prepares you for both public and private encounters. God has set positive aspects of success within each of us:

- Popularity – socialization and esteem.
- Promotion – advancement and achievement.
- Prosperity – it's great to be blessed right where you are.
- Productivity – the blessing of hard work is having good results.

There is never a time God does not know where you've been or where you're trying to go! The good news is that He is ready to lock us into the pattern of His promise.

Whither shall I go from thy spirit? or whither shall I flee from thy presence? If I ascend up into heaven, thou art there: if I make my bed in hell, behold, thou art there. If I take the wings of the morning, and dwell in the uttermost parts of the sea; even there shall thy hand lead me, and thy right hand shall hold me. If I say, Surely the darkness shall cover me; even the night shall be light about me. Yea, the darkness hideth not from thee; but the night shineth as the day: the darkness and the light are both alike to thee (Psalm 139:7-12).

The *"wings of the morning"* are in reference to the rays of the morning sun that streak across the heavens from east to west at 186,000 miles per second. Even if we could travel to some remote corner of the universe at the speed of light, we would find the Lord there, waiting to guide and uphold us.

God is absolutely inescapable. As Pascal, the French philosopher, explained, "His center is everywhere; His circumference is nowhere."

Oh, What Favor!

At some point it makes sense to acknowledge that your life is overflowing with constant acts of God's favor!

We are the spiritual descendants of those to whom favor is nothing new.

What the breeze is to wind!
What cold is to ice!
What heat is to fire!
What honey is to a bee,
What wet is to water,
What sweet is to sugar
That's what you are to favor!

When I finally realize God's love, His love pulls me deeper into relationship! I'm in so deep that I know I am covered even when He is constraining me! I'm swallowed up in favor!

---

*Sinners hide from God, but
believers hide in God.*

Start Walking in Your Assignment

Please understand that when the Lord is working on your behalf, He sanctifies and consecrates you to Him—and this is not for anyone else. God is preparing you for the work He plans to do in your life.

Those who are attached to you may have a variety of reactions. Some are discouragers who mock and murmur at what God is doing, while others are encourages who are excited to be watching your progress.

Please know that God will not give you victory until you step out in faith and start walking in your assignment. I've met those who long to win, but don't want to put in the effort required to run the race. When it comes to your destiny it's not a matter of picking and choosing what seems the easiest path. You have to run the entire race.

STIR UP YOUR GIFT

Righteousness must be an umbrella over your entire existence. You can't randomly choose when you want God's help and when you don't. In your relationship with the Lord, He must be over everything you think and do.

God knows your thoughts and won't excuse your lack of participation. He expects you to use the gifts He has given.

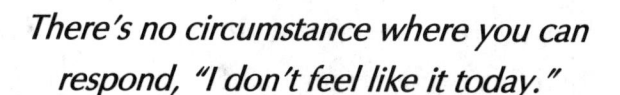

There's no circumstance where you can respond, "I don't feel like it today."

He doesn't tell you, "I will stir up your gift." Rather, He says, *"...stir up your gift of God, which is in thee"* (2 Timothy 1:6).

The decision rests with you alone. You can stir it up for right or wrong. However, when the Lord wants to bless you, He will remove the obstacles in your path. Remember He is constantly watching every move you make. As the Bible declares, *"Neither is there any creature that is not manifest in his sight: but all things are naked and opened unto the eyes of him"* (Hebrews 4:13).

His knowledge is so inconceivable that He can guard and protect us from behind and in front.

Even when we try to slip away, He still knows exactly where we are.

The Lord may allow you to wander off course, but if you ask Him, He will bring you back into the fold.

It's Happening in You!

For a moment imagine what the church would be like if people arrived on Sunday and announced, "I've been fasting, praying, and seeking God all week long."

What would happen if the members never uttered one curse word, told a lie, gossiped, or harbored lust? Think of the spiritual explosion that would take place in your home if you dedicated one week to total sanctification and living right in the eyes of God.

Since the Lord deserves your whole life, one week shouldn't be that difficult.

Can you suppress your anger and love your enemies for seven days?

Think of the possibilities when you realize that something marvelous is happening *in* you.

2

THE POWER OF PASSION

O God, thou art my God; early will I seek thee: my soul thirsteth for thee, my flesh longeth for thee in a dry and thirsty land, where no water is; to see thy power and thy glory, so as I have seen thee in the sanctuary. Because thy lovingkindness is better than life, my lips shall praise thee.

– PSALM 63:1-3

The word *passion* by itself is the catalyst for getting things done, but I also see it as a reason why many things aren't being accomplished as effectively as they should be.

It is important to know that there is a power associated with what God has given us to do—and it is tied to the drive or the "will" the Lord pushes us towards.

Far too often our desire and "push" are in areas the Creator didn't design or plan for us to have it in. As followers of Christ we are first and foremost to be soul winners. If you don't carry any other calling as a believer you should at least know the Gospel of salvation and have a compelling desire for others to have the opportunity to know Jesus Christ as their personal Savior. However, to do this you must have your own passion for this Christian walk.

The key to the immediate freedom and independence you have toward your present and future is that you are free to visualize your destination—even when you are not yet there.

This is one of the major reasons we need passion. It has the power to propel us to places we ordinarily would not dare go.

When you have a great desire for the things of God there is a zeal that accompanies it.

In addition, there is a "stick to it" factor that motivates you to finish what you have been placed on this earth to do.

Without passion you will just be going through the

motions. This is why it is essential to have a burning desire to fulfill the calling of your life. In other words, there must be a power attached to your passion.

Plow Through Every Obstacle

What does a passion for God look like? It is an irresistible emotion, an insisting devotion, a relentless persistence, and an insatiable pursuance.

This means you will plow through every obstacle —determined to accomplish certain goals. This becomes so much a part of you that you won't have to worry about wavering on your assignment. Nothing can stop you.

Regarding the things of God, you need to be in a position with the Almighty that you never get enough of Him:

- Never get enough of serving.
- Never get enough of pleasing the Lord.
- Never get enough of what God has called you to do.

With a true passion in your soul you won't need anyone to pat you on the back or continually encourage you. You become a self-starter and a self-finisher.

Even though drive is in your passion, drive by itself does not have the intensity, urgency, or pull that is required.

FACING THE DARKNESS

Passion helps us conquer the dark areas of life. There are valleys we all go through at one time or another. During creation, the Bible tells us that *"darkness was on the face of the deep"* (Genesis 1:2).

Darkness is the custodian of blindness and is unique within itself. It can hide both a truth and a lie. When you can't see, you are forced to work your way through circumstances and you can only operate by the process of faith.

Suddenly, you find yourself in a place that is pregnant with the unexpected—and fear often sets in.

Have you ever walked into a pitch black room and slid your hand along a wall hoping to find the light switch you know is there? When you can't feel it, uncertainty sets in.

Perhaps in that same dark room you tripped over an object you thought you had navigated around. It's frustrating.

Well, we all have some dark areas in our lives where we need God's help to find our way. In many cases, the Lord is saying, "The answer is near, but you just can't see it yet. Keep pressing on until you are there." It is at this time you need enough faith to hold onto the promise God has for you.

Finding Your Way Out

There is an element of transition in darkness. It is not always doom; it may only be obscurity. Darkness allows us to hold onto what is hidden from view—and many don't realize they are clinging to these concealed things. In fact, most emotional crutches are realized in the dark.

---⟫---

There are many conditions people never recover from because they can't seem to find their way out.

Sadly, some individuals choose to stay in the dark regarding certain matters and don't ever want the light to shine on their deep-seated problem. Only God can deliver them.

I've known men and women who would rather keep truth tucked away in the dark than to know it's reality. They mess up, but pretend they didn't—because they have blocked truth from their minds. As a result they revert to the darkness of flesh and hide in their iniquity.

What happens next is even more tragic. Sin builds itself up until it overwhelms them. As David wrote, *"For my iniquities have gone over my head; like a heavy burden they are too heavy for me"* (Psalm 38:4 NKJV).

He had dealt with enough dirt that it almost buried him alive. It is why he cried out to God, *"Make haste to help me, O Lord, my salvation"* (verse 22).

If we are attached to darkness through sin, it will steal our openness to positive change.

THE CUSTODIAN OF EXPOSURE

Is your life stuck in darkness? If so, this is not where you belong. We are children of light. Therefore, to explore a dark place, God's mystery has to become our focal point—and His revelation must become the means of unraveling the mystery.

We have to tell the Lord, "Whatever You want me to see, reveal it so I can escape and move to where You want me to be. I'm trusting You to solve the problem."

Yes, darkness is the custodian of blindness, but light is the custodian of exposure.

Ask God to reveal His plan and purpose. You may be trapped in a particular situation, but all of a sudden you will see the answer clearer than the light of day.

As believers we must become observers—seeing what is happening spiritually around us. Ask the Lord to help you move and flow in His divine atmosphere.

A Zest for Life

We must develop a passion to know what God is saying about particular circumstances. But this hunger usually starts from a distance. Then, as your interest is awakened, you are hooked on the subject and want to know more and more.

The passion is always there—waiting for the excitement and emotion to join forces with it. Emotion is the invisible power source behind our will. It responds to our sensitivities and it ignites and fires up our motivation.

Passion for the future is what makes our tomorrows brighter.

When this zest for life is present, it compels you to seek an objective until it is revealed. You say to yourself, "I'm going after this until it's mine!"

Have you lost or lack true passion for God? If so, what are you doing to regain your first love?

If the only time you embrace how you truly feel about the Lord is when you go to church, there's something sadly missing. Loving God should be an everyday experience.

Take a clue from the psalmist. He begins, *"O God, thou art my God; early will I seek thee"* (Psalm 63:1).

He is saying. "Lord, every opportunity possible I am searching for Your presence. I will fellowship with You in my daily devotions and talk with You every hour."

This reflects drive, desire, and excitement—but without passion, these three are meaningless.

- Passion with drive gives momentum.
- Passion with desire produces endurance.
- Passion with excitement creates anticipation.

When these elements are combined, there will be a spiritual explosion!

Suddenly, there is meaning to life. Your dreams can give you a picture of hope, but you can only realize it by the passion and drive God has given you.

WHAT IS THE PURPOSE OF PASSION?

Passion increases your relationship with God and all things pertaining to Him. When it is present, being close to our heavenly Father becomes a matter of life or death.

The Lord reveals His vision for our future and gives us the appetite to go after it. This is why God will place a potential blessing in front of you, then restructure it to fit your ability to retrieve what He is offering.

The reason you have the favor of God at this moment is because He made situations fall in line so you could receive His blessings.

The Lord is able to make things come your way that are beyond your imagination—all because you have a deep desire for Him.

Reaching for God is effort well spent, while <u>hearing</u> from God adds tremendous value to our living!

I can tell you from personal experience that the Lord will take care of you beyond measure. All that is required is for you to a have a passion for the things of God. As Jesus declares, *"But seek ye first the kingdom of God, and his righteousness; and all these things shall be added unto you"* (Matthew 6:33).

Unfortunately, most people do just the opposite. They expect "things" without first seeking the Lord.

IGNITE THE FLAME

Right now, ask yourself, "How hot is my fire?"

Do you need a jump-start every time you come into an atmosphere of worship? Does somebody have to pray and encourage you through? Or is the flame constantly burning on the inside?

God has so much He longs to do for us, but is hindered by our lack of passion for Him. Would we keep showering gifts upon a person who isn't grateful?

If the Lord has blessed you in any way, you owe Him something in return.

There should be an urging inside that demands that you bless God like He blesses you.

Say with the psalmist: *"I will bless the Lord at all times: his praise shall continually be in my mouth"* (Psalm 34:1).

David is not just shouting or saying hallelujah! Rather, he is letting the world know that regardless of the situation, he will praise the Lord. This tells us we are to bless our friends and our enemies alike.

Scripture tells us to, *"...bless them that curse you, do good to them that hate you, and pray for them which despitefully use you"* (Matthew 5:44).

When you operate in kindness, your foes become paralyzed from attacking you. As Romans 12:20 reads,

"Therefore if thine enemy hunger, feed him; if he thirst, give him drink: for in so doing thou shalt heap coals of fire on his head."

Even if your adversaries want to retaliate, somehow they can't. Because of your goodness—being a grace-giver rather than a stone-thrower—you have protection from above.

RIGHT LIVING

Why reduce yourself to deeds and dispositions that are outside the will of God? Allow people to see the fruit of the Spirit in action.

Always walk in the path of righteousness. *"For the Lord God is sun and shield: the Lord will give grace and glory: no good thing will he withhold from them that walk uprightly"* (Psalm 84:11)

If someone gets on your nerves or even clouds your reputation with lies, just keep walking on the right path.

Never lose your passion to live a holy life before a holy God. Remember, *"Blessed are they which do hunger and thirst after righteousness: for they shall be filled"* (Matthew 5:6).

I pray you will make it your aim to be so consumed with God's love and power that the enemy stays clear of you. The next time someone tries to heap verbal garbage or foolishness on you, respond with, "I'm too filled with the Spirit to have time for this conversation!"

Are you thirsty for the exciting future God has planned?

---◈---

When your hunger and thirst becomes unbearable, you aren't far from your next blessing.

God's Blueprint

Your passion will stir up your potential. In fact, your potential has no stock in your past when all of God's hope is invested in your future.

In addition, passion brings out intelligence in your discipline—and your discipline gives your passion a sense of order.

When you live according to God's blueprint, your zeal for certain objectives begins to make sense. You will receive more and more answers along the way until your goal is within reach.

I constantly advise and warn people not to put their energy in the wrong place. If you do, it starts to aggravate you.

When God begins to show you who you really are

and where you are supposed to go, when things are out of sync with His will, you will know it and feel uncomfortable.

If the activity it's not attached to your future, why waste your time?

Of course, there will be occasions when God will have to give you grace to deal with those who want to separate you from your passion.

You'll quickly learn what and who you can and cannot be involved with. The Lord will set the boundaries and tell you how far you can go. There will even be moments when God tells you when to stop so you won't cast your pearls before swine (Matthew 7:6).

He will reveal the true motives of others and help you avoid relationship traps.

Be open and allow the Lord to use you. For example, an individual may be going through a crisis and God will ask you to become their answer. You may not understand it at the time, but if you are sensitive to the voice of the Lord, be ready to respond and obey. He will give you discernment.

God will lead you to people who need Him—even if they are not aware of what is taking place.

At other times, the Lord may give you a clear signal to say "No"—even to a friend or family member. You will know it is of God if there is a deep peace in your soul concerning the matter. It is the *"...peace of God, which passeth all understanding"* (Philippians 4:7).

Your Time Is Coming!

Be sure you have a passion for the "right stuff."
We can easily mess up by jumping in on a good idea that is not part of your God-given assignment.

The Lord doesn't make you an ambulance chaser, so don't become one.

In addition, seek God's face regarding personal investments and money matters. There will always be wickedness in the world of finances.

Never be in a rush to attain riches. Your time is coming. Remember, *"...the wealth of the sinner is laid up for the just"* (Proverbs 13:22).

Be confident of who you are in God. When you fully know your position in Him, you won't worry about the "crunch" or the dark valley. You'll realize it is just a detour on the way to peace.

Start living like David, who said, *"I have been young, and now am old; yet have I not seen the righteous forsaken, nor his seed begging bread"* (Psalm 37:25).

If God can clothe the lilies in the field and feed the sparrows in the trees (Matthew 6:16-29), what makes you doubt the same God will not take care of you?

"I'm Going to Have It!"

Starting today, stir up your future while you are in your present. Tell the Lord:

- "I feel my passion getting stronger!"
- "Everything God says I can do, I'm going to accomplish!"
- "Everything God says is mine, I'm going to have!"

You are responsible for the:

- Blessing that is in your hands.
- Knowledge that is in your head.
- Compassion that is in your heart.
- Gifting that is on your life.
- Thirst that is in your desire.
- Hunger that is in your soul.

If you are in a constant, right relationship with the Lord, when you go to church God should be speaking the things that you have been talking to Him about—proclaiming His promises and declaring His Word.

Let revelation flow from your lips as God speaks and reveals His will to you.

Regarding the Lord's voice, far too many believers have a nonchalant, "catch it when it comes" attitude. You shouldn't simply be catching it, you need to be sending it—speaking the revelation He is giving.

Your passion reveals the true treasure of your inner man. As the Bible tells us, *"...for out of the abundance of the heart the mouth speaketh"* (Matthew 12:34).

Stagnation or procrastination will keep you from what you truly treasure. Pursue the desire of your heart regardless of what those around you may say.

TRUE INFLUENCE

Passion will cause your influence to meet your purpose. To express it another way, until influence meets purpose, it is not real influence.

Many have powers of persuasion they don't use—and as a result they fail to tap into their reason for being.

If we have a deep yearning for what God has called us to do, when we start moving towards it all of our tools and skills will rise to the surface. They will help shape our calling and bring it into reality.

- From the moment you begin to breathe you immediately have the authority to do something.
- From the moment you learn to think and believe what God says, you have the power to start something.
- From the moment you start talking and have faith, you have the voice to say something.

So don't just sleep on your opportunity. Your purpose is crying out for action, creativity, and for the sound of your voice.

Never go through life simply inhaling and exhaling. Make things happen!

THE BENEFITS OF PASSION

What we are talking about is much more than a feeling or a desire. Passion has benefits.

God is not just <u>with</u> you, He is also <u>in</u> you.

On the Day of Pentecost, there was an infilling of His Spirit (Acts 2:1-4). This means that as Christians we have no excuse for not being better than a carnal man. If carnality is the best we can achieve, we are living far beneath our privilege.

We must not allow our actions to be tied to the flesh. You have too much of God inside and you are a spiritual being. As a result, there should be manifestations of the Spirit in your life.

Sure, there are circumstances which will pop up in the natural that you can handle in the flesh, but it is imperative that your spiritual man take precedence over the natural whenever possible. As a result, your life will be a living testimony that pleases God.

It's Beginning to Rain!

You have blessings headed your way that you can't see coming!

I love the story of the prophet Elijah and his servant Gehazi regarding what happened after a three-and-a-half year drought.

> *And Elijah said unto Ahab, Get thee up, eat and drink; for there is a sound of abundance of rain. So Ahab went up to eat and to drink. And Elijah went up to the top of Carmel; and he cast himself down upon the earth, and put his face between his knees, and said to his servant [Gehazi], Go up now, look toward the sea. And he went up, and looked, and said, There is nothing.*

And he said, Go again seven times. And it came to pass at the seventh time, that he said, Behold, there ariseth a little cloud out of the sea, like a man's hand. And he said, Go up, say unto Ahab, Prepare thy chariot, and get thee down that the rain stop thee not (1 Kings 18:41-44).

The lesson from this story that we need to learn and practice is that we must run in the direction of our blessing!

A Great Shout!

Never be embarrassed or afraid to let your emotions show. Go ahead and shout!

When God gave Joshua the plan for capturing Jericho, he was to march with his army around the walls of the city once each day for six days. But on the seventh day, they were to circle Jericho seven times, then at a precise moment, *"...when the priests blew with the trumpets, Joshua said unto the people, Shout; for the Lord hath given you the city"* (Joshua 6:16).

The shout was so intense that the walls of Jericho fell flat and the armies of Israel marched in.

Victory lives in the shout of the elect!

It's Time to Celebrate

When you realize what the Lord has accomplished in and through your life, it's time to celebrate with praise.

Praising reinforces our spiritual foundation and reminds us of our past victories.

Testifying of God's goodness recounts His favor and encourages us with the fact that He is able to do it again. It also releases His great exploits.

You praise Him because:

- Simplicity brings clarity.
- Innocence brings grace.
- Faith releases your dreams.
- Depending on Him gets your needs met.
- Humility brings elevation.

Giving the Lord praise allows heaven to measure our affection toward Him. It reveals that we still trust Him with our hearts.

Praise God until you sense the aroma of worship, have the scent of victory, and know you are in the atmosphere of His divine presence.

When we praise our Creator it breaks any selfish authority we may have. Even more, when we publically sing, dance, and shout before the Lord it does away with any shame we may harbor.

Your Praise is powerful enough to:

- Shake kings and governments.
- Hold back judgment.
- Call down fire from heaven.
- Manifest joy in depression.
- Conquer and overcome defeat.
- Bring down the walls.

Psalm 47:1 tells us to *"...shout unto God with the voice of triumph."*

The walls of adversity cannot stand when your passion meets your praise. So go ahead and joyfully praise Him!

3

TIME TO JOIN THE "HAPPY PEOPLE"

Blessed be the Lord my strength [rock] which teacheth my hands to war, and my fingers to fight: my goodness [mercy], and my fortress; my high tower, and my deliverer; my shield, and he in whom I trust; who subdueth my people under me. Lord, what is man, that thou takest knowledge of him! or the son of man, that thou makest account of him! Man is like to vanity: his days are as a shadow that passeth away. Bow thy heavens, O Lord, and come down: touch the mountains, and they shall smoke. Cast forth lightning, and scatter them: shoot out thine arrows, and destroy them. Send thine hand from above; rid me, and deliver me out of great waters, from the hand of strange children; whose mouth speaketh vanity, and their right hand is a right hand of falsehood.

— PSALM 144:1-8

*I will sing a new song unto thee, O God:
upon a psaltery and an instrument of ten
strings will I sing praises unto thee. It is he
that giveth salvation [victory] unto kings: who
delivereth David his servant from the hurtful
sword. Rid me, and deliver me from the hand
of strange children, whose mouth speaketh vanity,
and their right hand is a right hand of falsehood:
that our sons may be as plants grown up in their
youth; that our daughters may be as corner stones,
polished [cut] after the similitude of a palace: that
our garners may be full, affording all manner of
store: that our sheep may bring forth thousands,
and ten thousands in our streets: that our oxen
may be strong to labour; that there be no
breaking in, nor going out; that there be no
complaining in our streets. Happy is that
people, that is in such a case: yea happy
is that people, whose God is the Lord.*

— PSALM 144:9-15

Most men, women, and children have a difficult time in this game of life if they are not personally happy. Their gloomy outlook eventually produces arguments, broken relationships, even legal battles.

There are millions who go through their entire journey on earth searching for happiness—whether in a person, a career, an objective, or even trying to find satisfaction in themselves.

I've met those who say, "If you just live by the rules and regulations, your worries will be over."

Well, if we look at the children of Israel, they certainly had their problems. Yes, they were given the Ten Commandments as rules for life, and had a 40-year journey through the wilderness to put them into practice, yet they grumbled and complained constantly.

RULES FOR LIVING

The commandments given by God to Moses (Exodus 20:1-17) were broken into two segments.

The first three deal with man's relationship with God:

1. You shall have no other gods before Me.
2. You shall not worship idols.
3. You shall not misuse the name of the Lord, your God.

The last seven deal with God's relationship with man:

4. Remember the Sabbath day and keep it holy.
5. Honor your father and mother.
6. You shall not murder.
7. You shall not commit adultery.
8. You shall not steal.
9. You shall not give false testimony against your neighbor.
10. You shall not covet.

These commandments were given to create order and morality—allowing us to function and be content on the earth. But even with these simple rules for living, people disobey and experience conflict.

Man's Search for Happiness

When you live right and find happiness in one area of your life, you'll find it spreads to practically everything else you do. The opposite is also true. Negative thoughts turn into negative actions that will affect you emotionally and physically. For example if you hate your job situation, you may find your eating habits going downhill too.

So how is happiness defined? The world has been searching for the answers for all of recorded history.

Here are several realms of thought:

Hedonism: This was a practice written about by Aristippus, a student of Socrates. It says that pleasure is the aim of life and its highest good. Later, Epicurus stated that intellectual pleasure is better because it is more lasting, but we cannot do without pleasure of the senses. The ultimate theme of hedonism rests in the adage, "If it feels good, do it!"

Utilitarianism: Jeremy Bentham, a political and legislative reformer in England, embraced the theory that moral goodness is an act to be judged by its utility in promoting the common welfare of all as well as the personal advantage of each. The greatest happiness includes the greatest number (or the majority). In this philosophy, being adopted and accepted by the masses is more important than being individually right. Anything which promotes this hierarchy is said to be the primary target of happiness!

Stoicism: This avenue of thought states that virtue is the only good. It is a disposition of the mind that is always consistent and harmonious. The virtuous man stands firm though the world crashes about him, realizing his identity with nature—and that he is beyond good and evil. In this view, virtue is above happiness and is not only attached to nature and God (pantheism), but also fate and destiny (fatalism).

Evolutionism: This does not refer to the biological theories of the 19th century. Rather, it is an ideology developed by Herbert Spencer, a philosophical prophet. He stated that adjustment produces pleasure, lack of it produces pain! His thought is that ancestral experiences of pleasure and pain are transmitted through brain modifications and accumulated through many generations. We thus inherit ethical habits, doing now through a sense of duty what our ancestors found pleasant or useful.

By the way, psychologist and educational reformer John Dewey refutes environmentalism with what he termed *instrumentalism*. This says that thinking is functional and value is in whatever a man finds satisfaction in doing. For most people, however, it is easier to travel than to arrive.

More than Surface Teaching

Today, we live in a culture that wants instant

happiness. Even in the church world, if you don't have a quick, simplistic approach, people will go elsewhere. It is difficult to teach "the deep things of God."

Many want a light message or surface instruction that tells them everything is going to be all right.

At some point, however, there is a spiritual hunger that cries out for the wisdom and insight of God's Word. There should be a cry from within that says, "I cannot settle for less."

We need something solid we can digest—that will take us to the place God has planned.

EMPTY HEARTS AND WEARY SOULS

It's important to pay attention to what our children are learning—both educationally and spiritually. My heart aches when I see young people go away to college and return questioning their faith.

Often they become mixed up and disillusioned because we haven't given them parameters to understand the different onslaughts of thoughts and concepts they would face.

Yes, they will be bombarded by the philosophies we have mentioned, but will such concepts bring true happiness? There are millions who can answer, "No."

Unrestrained, wild living leads to an empty heart and a weary soul. Trying to find satisfaction by running with the crowd is futile. Even virtuous mind training, positive thinking, and staying in touch with yourself has its limits.

Chasing the world's ideas leads to frustration and disappointment. I'm sure there have been times when you thought some particular experience was going to make you happy, but you ended up being miserable.

Countless people search and never find. They flip from one objective to the next, always starting new projects and never finishing the old ones.

If there was a scorecard of achievements it would be filled with the word "incomplete."

We have no special faculty in our being called "pleasure," because our enjoyment must be attached to something greater than ourselves. This is what makes it come alive.

True Contentment

In the psalms, David tells us that happiness will be found in serving our King—our Rock of Strength. The only true pleasure in life is to find contentment in God. Without a heart, mind, and soul relationship with your Creator, you will never know what joy is all about. In Psalm 144:2, David addresses the Lord with five titles: He is:

1. My *"goodness"*—steadfast love, mercy, compassion, and favor.
2. My *"fortress"*—my stronghold, citadel, and bastion.
3. My *"high tower"*—my high place, security, refuge, and defense.
4. My *"deliverer"*—my liberator, emancipator, the One who sets me free.
5. My *"shield"*—my protector, safeguard, or shelter.

Although each of these metaphors is interesting, one that stands out is *fortress*. David uses a unique Hebrew word *metsûdah*, which is translated "hold" in 1 Samuel 24:22 and 1 Chronicles 12:8. Many scholars believe that when David took flight from King Saul, his men and he sought safety at the fortress of Masada, "the hold." Masada is located about two and one-half miles from the western shore of the Dead Sea and is a plateau imposingly rising about 1,300 feet from the valley below.

In the mind of the psalmist, perhaps no better physical fortress could be referred to in depicting the strength of Jehovah on his behalf.

The psalmist probably wrote this in his later years. He seems to be recounting past mercies of the Lord for the benefit of his posterity.

WE ARE WEAK BUT HE IS STRONG

In verses 3 and 4 of this psalm (NKJV), David lets us know that as mortals we are puny and weak. He talks about:

- Our meagerness: *"Lord, what is man that You take knowledge of him?"*
- Our mortality: *"Man is like a breath...a passing shadow."*

Man's insignificance and transitory nature enhance the marvel of God's gracious care for him. We are but a mere shadow that quickly passes away.

Next, God prepares David for battle (verses 5-8). David prays that the Almighty will appear in His majesty and deliver him from his treacherous enemies. With lightning as his arrows, Yahweh is asked to scatter and destroy his foes. He requests God to put forth His hands to rescue him out of "many waters"—dangers at the hands of foreign enemies who swear to falsehood and cannot be trusted.

Radical Faith

Personally, I've been through many challenges, but the only place I have truly found happiness is when I allow God to rule my life.

As David tells us, if you want to know real delight, don't look for it in an earthly person or material possessions, but in your heavenly Father.

In the first few verses of this psalm, God is helping David deal with his enemies, but then he begins to pray for the prosperity of the people. This tells us that if we have radical faith we can expect remarkable results.

When you give God your total trust, He will bring *"joy unspeakable and full of glory"* (1 Peter 1:8). There will be outcomes you did not anticipate.

Is it of God?

Today, you are likely to hear advice from a variety of

individuals, some who believe they, like David, have a prophetic gift. But we have to prayerfully decipher what is of God and what is not. Most people, however, talk far more about their own issues—and what they are going through—than your situation. So if their counsel doesn't ring true, don't be afraid to politely say, "Thank you, but I don't think that pertains to me."

Remember this: all prophecy must be attached to the Word of God. If someone says, "The Lord is telling me this"—it needs to be verified in Scripture. It should be in line with what God is saying.

What you are experiencing should be connected to what you have been praying for and asking the Lord to do. Your objective should not be about cars, homes, or relationships, but about discovering God's will for your life. When this is primary, all the other blessings will come in His timing.

The Lord will show you what your obligations are and what actions you must take to accomplish His will.

As you study the Old Testament, the prophets were disciplined. After they were in the wilderness, denying themselves with fasting and prayer, they heard from the

Almighty and brought the message to specific people.

Today, if we expect to operate in the supernatural, we need that discipline too. We must walk in tune with the Word and become part of the five-fold ministry as an apostle, prophet, evangelist, pastor, or teacher (Ephesians 4:11).

As a believer, there is no greater satisfaction than to be in the center of God's perfect will.

You should constantly be talking with Him concerning what He wants to see happen through you in the days ahead.

The Blame Game

Where you are and where you are headed must be between you and God. Never fall into the trap of blaming others for not achieving your goals—whether they are material or spiritual. So often, when things aren't going our way in our search for happiness, we say it was someone else's fault.

Let me identify four types of blame:

1. Ordinary Blame

This involves basic accusation, projecting fault, and/or causing distraction without cause. In this case, you do not have a reason to accuse another person—you just don't want to own up for it yourself.

2. Irresponsible Blame

Now we're getting more serious—defacing someone's character, accusing an individual with no regard for the consequences. You don't care who you destroy or the results of your accusation.

3. Jealous Blame

Envy is a deadly cancer that spreads when you covet the person or object you accuse. This is an inordinate attraction and affection! When you blame life's consequences on who you share yourself with, it's Adamic in nature. You make others the object of your negative affection. In the process you make yourself a victim. Recognize the roots of jealousy and destroy them.

4. Righteous Blame

When you deliberately take credit for what others have done, your pride will eventually catch up with you. Don't hesitate to let others know the part they play in

INTENTIONAL LIVING

your success. If they opened a door for you, or helped in any way, express your appreciation. Give credit where credit is due!

How dare we unrighteously act as if we made it on our own. It not only robs someone else of happiness, it robs you too.

Right now, reflect back and identify a few individuals who helped you along your journey. Try some retroactive encouragement. Pick up the phone or write them a note and express your sincere gratitude.

THE REDEEMED MUST REJOICE!

Your next victory should not be a surprise. Anticipate what God is about to do. Instead of "blaming" Him, you will be blessing Him.

Finally, take joy in the fact that where you are at the present moment is not where you are going to stay.

God is about to match your request with His favor. Not because He has to, but because He can!

After David gives a prophecy concerning the

blessings of God that will fall on the righteous, he concludes with a song of victory. *"I will sing a new song unto thee, O God"* (Psalm 144:9).

Because God is so good, the redeemed of the Lord must rejoice! David promises to give thanks for the victory which he is confident will be granted. Such a new manifestation of God's grace will require a "new song." Yahweh is the God who gives "salvation" or victory to kings, and to David his servant in particular. The *"hurtful sword"* here (verse 10) is the calamity of war. Having expressed this confidence, David repeats the prayer of verses 7 and 8.

In addition, the redeemed of the Lord will be rewarded with the promises of God. This will happen:

- IN THE HOMES: *"That our sons may be as plants grown up in their youth; that our daughters may be as pillars, sculptured in palace style"* (Psalm 144:12 NKJV).

- IN THE FIELDS: *"That our barns may be full supplying all kinds of produce; that our sheep may bring forth thousands and ten thousands in our fields; that our oxen may be well laden"* (verses 13-14 NKJV).

- IN THE STREETS: *"That there be no breaking in or going out; That there be no outcry in our streets"* (verse 14:NKJV).

This inspiring psalm concludes with an affirmation of the happiness of God's people. The Lord is the source and sum of all true joy—temporal and eternal. *"Happy are the people who are in such a state; happy are the people whose God is the Lord!"* (Psalm 155:15 NKJV).

I pray you have joined the throng of God's "Happy People."

4

Improved, Impressive, and Magnificently Designed!

Now also when I am old and grayheaded, O God, forsake me not; until I have shewed thy strength unto this generation, and thy power to every one that is to come. Thy righteousness also, O God, is very high, who hast done great things: O God, who is like unto thee! Thou, which hast shewed me great and sore troubles, shalt quicken me again, and shalt bring me up again from the depths of the earth. Thou shalt increase my greatness, and comfort me on every side.

– Psalm 71:18-21

There are many viewpoints on how man was created. Some have mud being stretched out like a canvas on the ground, then God forming Adam into the framework of his actual existence. However, most biblical scholars suggest that man was created standing upright—as a mark of his governing authority.

In his poem, *The Creation,* James Weldon Johnson, educator and early civil rights activist, wrote:

> Up from the bed of the river
> God scooped the clay;
> And by the bank of the river
> He kneeled him down;
> And there the great God Almighty
> Who lit the sun and fixed it in the sky,
> Who flung the stars to the most far corner of the night,
> Who rounded the earth in the middle of His hand;
> This great God,
> Like a mammy bending over her baby,
> Kneeled down in the dust
> Toiling over a lump of clay
> Till he shaped it in is his own image;
> Then into it he blew the breath of life,
> And man became a living soul.

The earth however, had little to do with man's formation. It was God who shaped man in His own image. And since Adam was to have dominion over the earth, he was given the ability to walk and move about.

This being the case, man had to learn how to bow, to lie prostrate, even how to curl up in a fetal position. All this was necessary:

- If he never learned to bow, he would never learn to submit or to serve.
- If he never learned to lie prostrate, he would never learn to surrender or learn to rest.
- If he never learned to curl up, he would never learn to be vulnerable—or find security within his soul.

For these reasons—from the first man until today—we are always in the process of being improved. As the psalmist writes, *"Thou shalt increase my greatness, and comfort me on every side"* (Psalm 71:21).

———————— ◆》 ————————

The Lord not only desires to restore you to exceptional living, He will increase it! You will be better than before.

You'll not only experience comfort, but will be surrounded by it on every side. There will be no threats from any direction.

Like Job, there will be times when God will allow troubles to come our way. But remember, they are meant to advance our progress. So when problems appear, instead of complaining, start rejoicing!

———————⟫———————

Since we are children of God, we are improved, impressive, and magnificently designed.

Prepare for a Promotion

It is vital to understand who you are so you won't accept less than you deserve. Greatness has been deposited into your existence.

Go ahead and begin to reign where God has given you the power to rule. However, if you are not righteously fit for such authority, it is unreasonable to expect success. When you are not right with your Maker, you might be able to step into places of leadership, but you won't stay there long.

Based on how we prepare ourselves for the promotion God is ready to give us will determine the length of our reign.

David is thinking as an elder statesman as he writes, *"...when I am old and grayheaded"* (Psalm 71:18)—then he expresses his desire to share his life's wisdom and teach the principles of longevity.

Earlier in the same psalm, he says:

> *For thou art my hope, O Lord God: thou art my trust from my youth. By thee have I been holden up from the womb: thou art he that took me out of my mother's bowels: my praise shall be continually of thee. I am as a wonder unto many; but thou art my strong refuge. Let my mouth be filled with thy praise and with thy honour all the day.*
>
> – PSALM 71:5-8

The psalmist is letting his Creator know, "Lord, just as I needed You then, I still need You right now!" And he adds, *"O God, thou hast taught me from my youth: and hitherto have I declared thy wondrous works"* (verse 17).

From an early age, we must declare that everything the Lord does for us is marvelous. By saying, *"I am a wonder unto many,"* David recognizes the fact that there is no earthly explanation for why and how God blesses him the way He does! God's works are wondrous, and David is one of the wonders of His works!

We need to make it our business to declare the Lord's goodness to everyone we come in contact with!

Shaping Lives

David teaches us to insist that this generation learns to trust God, beginning in their youth—not to wait until they are fully mature.

Our focus must be on preparing our children and young people for a life of spiritual excellence.

This is why I treasure the presence of a child in the sanctuary. They are being exposed to the things of God that will mold and shape their future. They too are improved, impressive, and magnificently designed.

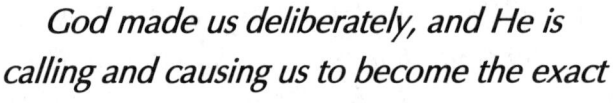

God made us deliberately, and He is calling and causing us to become the exact picture of what He envisions.

Far too many believe their dreams will never come to pass—that they will never find joy, completeness, and fulfillment.

One of the best things we can do for an impatient generation is to remind them that tomorrow will be better than today. Life is not over until God says so—it's only beginning.

As long as we have breath in our body, the future is on our side.

This is why we need to agree with David, *"For thou art my hope, O Lord God."* (Psalm 71:5).

- God will use favor to keep your hope alive.
- Confirmation will solidify your hope.
- Testimony will renew your hope.
- Experience will recall your hope.
- Favor will manage your hope.

Many of us do not realize it, but we are living in miracle territory! Always remember that God can use your "leftovers" and turn them into something spectacular.

These words are well worth repeating: it's never over until God says so.

Total Trust

The more we teach children to trust God, the stronger their faith and wisdom will be as they grow older.

We cannot afford to pacify the circumstances of life that demand immediate trust in the Lord. Let's not forfeit these moments by doubting the fact that God can do everything He promises. Remember, we walk by faith, not by sight.

The Almighty can and must be trusted:

- Trust is internal; it never comes from outside of us!
- Trust is a decision; it comes by opportunity and choice!
- Trust demands submission; you have to release doubt and fear to receive it.
- Trust only respects trial; if you won't try it you can't operate in its fulness.

Believing God doesn't free us from the attack of our accusers, rather it means we trust that He will protect and cover us in every situation.

Cast me not off in the time of old age; forsake me not when my strength faileth. For mine enemies speak against me; and they that lay wait for my soul take counsel together, saying, God hath forsaken him: persecute and take him; for there is none to deliver him. O God, be not far from me: O my God, make haste for my help. Let them be confounded and consumed that are adversaries to my soul; let them be covered with reproach and dishonour that seek my hurt.

– PSALM 71:9-13

A SPIRIT OF ENCOURAGEMENT

It's unfair for us to walk with God and leave others wandering in the wilderness of immaturity. We need to give them every opportunity to enjoy the goodness and greatness of our wonderful Lord.

Go ahead and release the spirit of encouragement to those around you. We have an obligation to see more than just ourselves set free. Create an atmosphere of liberty and freedom so that others can escape the bondage of the enemy.

Many young people "act out" and become reckless in their behavior because they have not been taught how to find their freedom in Christ. Freedom doesn't mean trying to force people to live within the boxes and framework of our own ideas. I've met Christian's who tell me, "I'm free," yet are moping around and complaining about whatever comes their way.

It's no wonder that some young people reject this idea, saying, "If that's what freedom looks like, count me out! I feel freer than that right now."

Every believer has to find his or her own liberty in God.

SELF-CONTROL

David tells us again and again that God must be trusted throughout our entire life. This may mean restructuring and reshaping our lives to conform to the image of our Maker. If we have blown it, thank God, we can be restored.

Ask the Lord to forgive you—then change your behavior so you won't repeat your mistakes and have to repent again. Let God give you the self-control and determination to mirror His excellence in everything you do.

Permit me to me suggest you learn and practice this simple life motto:

I am discerning what the Lord wants me to do. I am also inclined to do it, the Spirit of God is providing the self-control in me to do it to the best of my ability. My only challenge is conquering any disagreement between what I am presently thinking and what am I believing at the same time!

BEYOND CONFUSION

We all go through challenges. Our thoughts fight against our actions. As the Apostle Paul stated, *"For what I will to do, that I do not practice; but what I hate, that I do"* (Romans 7:15 NKJV).

It's only natural to wonder why there are so many highs and lows, ups and downs, and conflicts between good and evil. If we aren't careful we'll become totally confused. As James observes, *"A double minded man is unstable in all his ways"* (James 1:8). In New Testament syntax, when the word mind (*nous*) is used it is often synonymous with heart (*cardia*). Thus, when the affections of our heart and the reasoning of our mind don't agree, we are being double minded!

We need to ask ourselves, "Do I trust what God says

is best for me?"

If you do, you will start making up your mind on spiritual matters and not allow others to determine and rule your responses. The Lord will take preeminence and there will be no more confusion.

Paul found the answer to his dilemma, the tug of war between right and wrong. He writes:

> *There is therefore now no condemnation to them which are in Christ Jesus, who walk not after the flesh, but after the Spirit. For the law of the Spirit of life in Christ Jesus hath made me free from the law of sin and death. For what the law could not do, in that it was weak through the flesh, God sending his own Son in the likeness of sinful flesh, and for sin, condemned sin in the flesh: that the righteousness of the law might be fulfilled in us, who walk not after the flesh, but after the Spirit* (Romans 4:1-4).

Improvement is Part of Your Nature

If you need a reason to trust God, just look at His record and resume on your behalf:

- Has He held you?
- Has He protected you?
- Has He made a way for you?
- Has He opened doors for you?
- Has He been your friend?
- Has He been on your side?
- Has He kept you alive?
- Has He provided for you?
- Has He shown you a more excellent way?

Even when you have disqualified yourself, He gives you mercy and provides a second chance. When you feel like you are going to falter, He reaches down and gives you the inner strength to stand tall. Whether you are up or down, He causes you to look improved, impressive, and magnificent.

What a mighty God we serve.

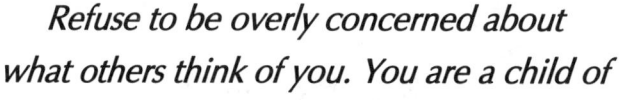

Refuse to be overly concerned about what others think of you. You are a child of the King, so start acting as such and be built up in the most holy faith.

You are fearfully and wonderfully made and the

Creator is not yet finished with you. Improvement is part of your nature.

God is lifting you up—not tomorrow but today. *"This is the day which the Lord has made; we will rejoice and be glad in it"* (Psalm 118:24).

The older I get the wiser I become in the things of God. What used to drive me crazy no longer bothers me. What once made me fall, now makes me smile. This is only possible because time with the Lord has given me spiritual strength and maturity.

Wisdom is released in the life of Christians through knowledge and experience. Faithful believers should automatically improve with age!

Words such as superb, excellent, brilliant, and marvelous should be staples in an ever-learning culture that embraces the knowledge of the truth in God!

Keep Praising!

One of the secrets of David's intimate relationship with God is that he didn't let hope outlast his praise. He writes, *"But I will hope continually, and will yet praise thee more and more. My mouth shall shew forth thy righteousness and thy salvation all the day; for I know not the numbers thereof. I will go in the strength of the Lord God: I will make mention of thy righteousness, even of thine only"* (Psalm 7:14-16).

- Your hope is pursuing the manifestation of your faith!
- Hope will drive you into expectation!
- Expectation will drive you into anticipation!
- Joyful anticipation will drive you into exuberant praise!

WITH YOUR HANDS, HEART, AND SOUL

David concludes this psalm by exclaiming:

I will also praise thee with the psaltery, even thy truth, O my God: unto thee will I sing with the harp, O thou Holy One of Israel. My lips shall greatly rejoice when I sing unto thee; and my soul, which thou hast redeemed. My tongue also shall talk of thy righteousness all the day long.
— PSALM 71:22-24

Above all of God's wonderful acts, the work of redemption must be celebrated by us in our praises.

How did David express his joy and exultation?

1. With his hand, in sacred music.

David excelled at playing the psaltery and the harp. He used the best of his skills to praise God and bring others into worship.

2. With his lips, in sacred songs.

When we make melody to the Lord by singing His praises, we use our lips and vocal cords, but the rejoicing must flow from our hearts. It is how "all that is within us" blesses His holy name."

3. With his soul, in sacred praise.

David was making music from, *"my soul, which thou hast redeemed."* Music produces a holy joy that is at the very core and life of thankful praise.

Greater than Anticipated

In this magnificent psalm, David exclaims:

- "I will run with all my might" (Psalm 71:9,20).
- "I treasure my experience in God" (verses 5, 6,17).
- "I still have challenges and pressures" (verses 4,13).
- "Yet I rely on prayer" (verses 1-9, 12-13).
- "I will always praise Him" (verses 8,14, 22-24).
- "I'm leaving the future up to God" (verses 18-21).

What you are about to experience in the Lord will be more than you expected and greater than you anticipated!

Like the psalmist, God will increase your greatness and comfort you on every side. Remember, you are improved, impressive, and magnificently designed!

5

CELEBRATE GREATNESS AND PASS IT ON!

I will extol thee, my God, O king; and I will bless thy name for ever and ever. Every day will I bless thee; and I will praise thy name for ever and ever. Great is the Lord, and greatly to be praised; and his greatness is unsearchable. One generation shall praise thy works to another, and shall declare thy mighty acts.
— PSALM 145:1-4

The psalms come in a variety of different forms. Some are Messianic, pointing to the coming Messiah; others are historical, dealing with the pattern and path

God took in delivering and guiding Israel.

Psalm 145 is one of praise for God's greatness.

There is also something very interesting about this particular psalm. It is written in the form of an acrostic—in that every verse begins with a successive letter of the Hebrew alphabet. We can find variations of acrostics in several others psalms including 9, 10, 37, and 119.

INFINITE GREATNESS

All 21 verses of Psalm 145 are total praise. Here, David is consumed with a holy determination to extol, bless, and praise his King daily and forever. This is not something he is doing occasionally, but continuously.

You can find many psalms where David was traveling through a deep valley before finding victory, but not this one. There is no "down in the dumps" or "crying myself to sleep" theme here. It's praise and worship from beginning to end.

You might find yourself singing right along with him—*"Great is the Lord, and greatly to be praised"* (Psalm 145:3).

The span of our God's greatness is infinite—without dimension. He is not just good some of the time, but always, and in every situation.

There are three indisputable facts about greatness!

1. God is great!
2. Every thought God has is great!
3. His thoughts produce His greatness!

One of the objectives of creation was to produce God's finished thought into an unfinished atmosphere! He had a picture of His desire—and spoke His plan into existence. It included mankind.

The more mature in God I become, the more I look like His original thought of me!

This is why our own thoughts must be totally centered on the things of God. As someone wisely wrote long ago:

> *Watch your thoughts, they become words,*
> *Watch your words, they become actions,*
> *Watch your actions, they become habits,*
> *Watch your habits, they become character,*
> *Watch your character, it becomes your destiny!*

Let the Whole World Know

In every verse of this psalm you can hear the heart of David:

One generation shall praise thy works to another, and shall declare thy mighty acts. I will speak of the glorious honour of thy majesty, and of thy wondrous works. And men shall speak of the might of thy terrible acts: and I will declare thy greatness. They shall abundantly utter the memory of thy great goodness, and shall sing of thy righteousness. The Lord is gracious, and full of compassion; slow to anger, and of great mercy. The Lord is good to all: and is tender mercies are over all his works. All thy works shall praise thee, O Lord; and thy saints shall bless thee.

—Psalm 145:4-10

If you ever have a difficult time getting started with your praise to the Lord, read this psalm. It will turn your attention from the distractions of the world and direct your thoughts to heaven.

It's a message you can't keep to yourself. You want

everyone to know what the Lord means to you.

The psalmist puts it this way: *"Every day will I bless thee; and I will praise thy name for ever and ever"* (Psalm 145:2).

As born again believers we can say "Thank You, Jesus":

- Every time we wake up.
- Every time we stand up.
- Every time we look up.
- Every time we speak up.

Why? Because God is blessing you in every area of your life. This is why you can express these words from your heart, *"I will bless the Lord at all times: his praise shall be continually in my mouth"* (Psalm 34:1).

NOTHING CAN COMPARE

David was God's choice to be King of Israel, but he extolled the Almighty as the *real* King. The word *extol* (Psalm 145:1) means exalt—to lift up and highly commend. It is wonderful when a king on earth recognizes that he is subservient to the King of heaven—that his own royalty can never compare with the King of kings and Lord of lords.

What David did, however, was to come into alignment with the Kingdom in order to fulfill God's plan.

Timeless Praise

The psalms were not only for the day in which they were written, they span the time of centuries and apply to us today. Seasons change, people are born and die, cultures come and go, but God's word is forever.

Praise is timeless and travels by the wind of the Spirit into the heavenlies. It is divine and eternal in nature. As you praise God it is part of your expectation of what is to come.

When you began your morning, I hope you told Him:

- "I praise You that I am awake again today."
- "I'm walking again."
- "I can hear again."
- "I can speak again."
- "I can see again."
- "I can feel again."
- "I can be fed again today."

Since there is a miracle taking place in your life right now and God is blessing you, go ahead and thank Him.

Instead of trying to find out where your next blessing is coming from, praise the Almighty for what He is currently doing. Hallelujah!

LET THE GENERATIONS KNOW

According to the Word, your praise to the Lord eventually becomes community property. As David tells us, *"One generation shall praise thy works to another, and shall declare thy mighty acts"* (Psalm 145:4).

- A father must tell his sons how good God is.
- A mother must tell her daughter how the Lord can make a way.
- A friend must tell another about the excellence of the Almighty.
- A believer ought to speak to another believer and rejoice in the Lord's goodness.

We are designed to partake in generational leadership! This is why we should never attempt to rush into the future!

When greatness appears, accommodations must be made for it! As the prophet Isaiah explains, *"Enlarge the place of thy tent, and let them stretch forth the curtains of thine habitations: spare not, lengthen thy cords, and strengthen thy stakes; for thou shalt break forth on the right hand and on the left; and thy seed shall inherit the Gentiles, and make the desolate cities to be inhabited"* (Isaiah 54:2-3).

It's time to occupy your territory. Use everything at your disposal—after all, faith is not conservative.

Your "right hand" is the authority you have through the Word of Truth! Your "left hand" is your authority through skill, knowledge, and integrity.

Where you are now is too confining for your dream! If you fail to increase your participation, your vision will suffocate and die! So go ahead and expand your borders, then fortify every inch of land you claim.

WHO WILL YOU SERVE?

We are not to be lazy or selfish and keep the blessings of God to ourselves. Rather, we are to pass them on. This is how every generation can know the greatness of the living Lord.

I think of what has happened to countless young people today. Many have been left to find their own way, with little input from their parents. As a result, we have millions who know how to rap, but don't know a thing about the rapture! They haven't been taught about the Redeemer.

As a pastor, I encounter the remnants of this generation who say, "The world has messed me up. I need to find God."

Our praise must become an example to others of our relationship with God and His Son, Jesus. After all, what we praise is usually our god—whether it is an earthly object or the true God of heaven. The Bible says, *"Choose ye this day whom ye will serve"* (Joshua 34:15). Who will that be? *"...but for me and my house, we will serve the Lord"* (verse 15).

It's Your Time

The psalmist gives us the origin of greatness. *"But our God is in the heavens: he hath done whatsoever he hath pleased"* (Psalm 115:3).

Yes, God is above all, but He also provides His children with the power to walk in this same greatness. As the Almighty told Job, *"Though thy beginning was small, yet thy latter end should greatly increase"* (Job 8:7).

Get ready to enter into your moment! Greatness is in you, yet you also need to make sure it is being developed in those around you. In other words, "Pass it on!"

From Greatness to Generosity

David ends this marvelous chapter with one more plea to let the world know of the mighty acts of God—and how close the Lord is to those who will call on His Name.

> *They shall speak of the glory of thy kingdom, and talk of thy power; to make known to the sons of men his mighty acts, and the glorious majesty of his kingdom. Thy kingdom is an everlasting kingdom, and thy dominion endureth throughout all generations. The Lord upholdeth all that fall, and raiseth up all those that be bowed down. The eyes of all wait upon thee; and thou givest them their meat in due season. Thou openest thine hand, and satisfiest the desire of every living thing. The Lord is righteous in all his ways, and holy in all his works. The Lord is nigh unto all them that call upon him, to all that call upon him in truth. He will fulfil the desire of them that fear him: he also will hear their cry, and will save them. The Lord*

preserveth all them that love him: but all the wicked will he destroy. My mouth shall speak the praise of the Lord: and let all flesh bless his holy name for ever and ever.

— Psalm 145:11-21

Let me encourage you to highlight this chapter in your Bible and read it again and again. You may even want to memorize certain verses and use them as daily affirmations of God's majesty.

Here is how we are to extol the Lord:

- For His greatness (Psalm 145:3).
- For His grace (verses 8,17).
- For His goodness (verse 9).
- For His glory (verses 11-12).
- For His generosity (verses 15-16).

Now is the time to celebrate God's greatness—and remember to pass it on!

6

GET READY TO TAKE OFF!

Praise ye the Lord. Praise ye the Lord from the heavens: praise him in the heights. Praise ye him, all his angels: praise ye him, all his hosts. Praise ye him, sun and moon: praise him, all ye stars of light. Praise him, ye heavens of heavens, and ye waters that be above the heavens. Let them praise the name of the Lord: for he commanded, and they were created. He hath also established them for ever and ever: he hath made a decree which shall not pass. Praise the Lord from the earth, ye dragons, and all deeps.

— PSALM 148:1-7

Fire, and hail; snow, and vapour; stormy wind fulfilling his word: mountains, and all hills; fruitful trees, and all cedars: beasts, and all cattle; creeping things, and flying fowl [birds of wing]: kings of the earth, and all people; princes, and all judges of the earth: both young men, and maidens; old men, and children: let them praise the name of the Lord: for his name alone is excellent [exalted]; his glory is above the earth and heaven. He also exalteth the horn of his people, the praise of all his saints; even of the children of Israel, a people near unto him. Praise ye the Lord.

— PSALM 148:8-14

I'm sure you've watched the televised countdown of a rocket launch from the Kennedy Space Center at Cape Canaveral. "Five Four Three Two One. Lift Off!"

This is exactly how I feel when I read Psalm 145. Something within me says this is a time of launching where God is being exalted, and so are his people. We are being raised to higher heights.

We all have the potential to reap an unusual harvest in our lives and reach into untapped fields of humanity!

Isn't it time to unlock your unused treasures? Will you begin searching through your present for things that belong to your future?

The elements of your increase could be much closer than you realize. They may include undeveloped and undiscovered riches you already possess.

Effortless Excellence

I am firmly convinced that every believer has a ministry. It's up to you to seek God until He reveals what you are placed on this earth to do.

When the Lord pulls back the curtain of heaven and shows you the vision He has created for you, don't hesitate to step into His plan.

Go ahead and acknowledge the demand for your ministry and realize that the world needs people of God who are moved by joy! And our joy should flow in effortless excellence.

I've seen the disastrous results that unfold when people have the wrong attitude. If individuals find themselves frustrated and angry in their service to God, it breeds a reaction of haughtiness, indignation, and coldness between people. It steals the balance and integrity of warm, honest, open communication. But when ministry is motivated by joy it releases a strength for healing *in* us and *through* us.

The apostle Paul exclaimed, *"Rejoice in the Lord always: and again I say, Rejoice"* (Philippians 4:4).

Never stop on your quest for joy. Lunge for it! Reach for it! Stretch out in it! I've seen what happens when you don't. The delight of ministry begins to disappear when you stop stretching your faith,

Most Christians walk by sight rather than by faith. They would prefer to be overly careful than step out into the deep and risk everything for God. Living by faith is not carelessness. It is being able to move freely in a non-judgmental and non-threatening spiritual atmosphere.

The Medicine of the Heart

Friend, be willing to drop your burdens! If you will release them into God's hands, He will take care of the rest. The psalmist tells us, *"The Lord taketh pleasure in them that fear Him, in those that hope in his mercy"* (Psalm 147:11). *"He brought forth his people with joy, and his chosen with gladness"* (Psalm 105:43).

It is impossible to successfully engage in ministry

without true joy—the medicine of the heart.

- Knowing God *unlocks* joy—allowing me to know Him better.
- Knowing His Word *reveals* joy—allowing me to love Him more.
- Trusting God *releases* joy—making life more pleasurable.
- Obeying God *restores* joy—renewing my strength.
- Praying to God *keeps* joy—keeping me encouraged.
- Praising God *stirs up* joy—increasing my praise.
- Worshiping God *fills me* with joy—making my worship addictive.

GOD-GIVEN IMAGINATION

Have you ever stopped to thank and praise the Lord for the mind He has placed within you? It's the most technically perfect computer in the world. We don't know how memory and focus works, yet we use them every day. In fact, almost all of our mental processing is involuntary. We automatically reason, construct, and reconstruct in the process of having things make sense.

Imagination is the mind's recreation and can take your thoughts to unbelievable destinations. Boredom, however, is a sign that your mind is crying out to either be used or to be entertained.

People tend to believe and practice what they can measure. This is why we don't have many dreams that live themselves out and become reality—because we are unfamiliar with our imagination!

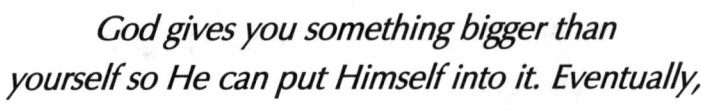

God gives you something bigger than yourself so He can put Himself into it. Eventually, He expects you to live up to the vision.

The world has learned to use imagination aggressively. Every night television stations tease you with small tidbits of information, then say, "News at 10." Magazines have tantalizing headlines on the cover to whet your appetite so you will buy a copy and look inside.

Our challenge with imagination is not our lack of using it, but our lack of control when imagination uses us!

God understands this and it is why the Word speaks so often of our mind. The psalmist tells us, *"The Lord knoweth the thoughts of man"* (Psalm 94:11). In fact, *"The Lord searcheth all hearts, and understandeth all the imaginations of the thoughts"* (1 Chronicles 28:9).

Our mind can be used for evil or for good. Scripture counsels, *"And be not conformed to this world: but be ye transformed by the renewing of your mind, that ye may prove what is that good, and acceptable, and perfect, will of God"* (Romans 12:2).

Faith uses your imagination because there is nothing in your intellect vast enough to contain the things of God—things your reasoning can't make sense of.

Your mind can only grasp small fragments of an awesome God who created and rules the universe.

THE CALL OF THE DEEP

Psalm 148 lets us know that everything is to praise God—sun, moon, stars, water, fire, wind, mountains, trees, cattle, birds, kings, princes, judges, men, women, and children,

We can also praise Him for what is unknown—*"the deep things of God"* (1 Corinthians 2:10).

David refers to this when he writes, *"Deep calleth unto deep at the noise of thy waterspouts: all thy waves and thy billows are gone over me"* (Psalm 42:7).

The sincere in heart will hear the call of the deep! David is giving an example of being under God's outpouring. At the point where the "pouring" hits the surface of the water, a spout is formed.

The noise caused by the force of the pouring is then echoed beneath the waters in the deep places. Yet there is something else taking place here. The deep hears what is happening on the surface but is unaffected by it. The deep is unmoved by surface winds of doctrine or trends of popularity, being grounded on foundation and only moved by flow!

In these words, God is giving us three dimensional pictures of sight:

- *Hindsight:* Praise in our experiences!
- *Insight:* Praise in our revelation!
- *Foresight:* Praise in our expectation!

Let me encourage you to seek divine insight.! Vision might be what we picture, but sight is *how much* of it we see!

New Heights

When the Lord is high and lifted up, you will be elevated too! Why? Because that is where you will be living. Remember, God inhabits the praises of His people!

You can echo the words of David: *"Praise the name of the Lord, for his name alone is exalted; his splendor is above the earth and the heavens. He has raised up for his people a horn, the praise of all his saints"* (Psalm 143:13-14 NIV).

I believe God is ready to raise you up to places you have never been and heights you have never reached. Get ready for lift off!

7

THEY PRAYED, THEY PRAISED, AND THEN THEY DANCED!

*Praise ye the Lord [literally Hallelujah!].
Sing unto the Lord a new song, and his praise in the congregation of saints. Let Israel rejoice in him that made him: let the children of Zion be joyful in their King. Let them praise his name in the dance: let them sing praises unto him with the timbrel and harp.*

— PSALM 149:1-3

If each of us is not taking time to praise God every day, there's something radically wrong. We have time to chat on the phone, watch reality shows on televison, play video games, and even gossip over the back fence. Where is the Lord in our lives? Why can't we carve out five minutes or more daily to stop what we are doing and get alone with God? I guarantee that if you will start praising Him for His goodness, you'll move into an entirely new atmosphere and dimension. Five minutes will turn into ten, then into twenty—and who knows how long you will spend in fellowship with Him.

The exciting part is that your communion with heaven will transform your behavior. You will soon look at yourself and say, "I've changed. I'm not practicing those old habits anymore."

Spiritually, many are in critical condition and don't even know the severity of their situation. Be aware that your life is not your own. Because of the work of Calvary, you were bought with a price. So begin to praise the Father for what you have received through His Son.

Seize these moments and glorify God with every part of your being.

Say "Hallelujah!"

Psalm 149 is called the "Hallelujah Psalm". It begins

with "Praise ye the Lord [Hallelujah]" (verse 1) and ends the exact same way. Together, let's look at the rest of this psalm:

> *For the Lord taketh pleasure in his people: he will beautify the meek with salvation. Let the saints be joyful in glory: let them sing aloud upon their beds. Let the high praises of God be in their mouth, and a twoedged sword in their hand; to execute vengeance upon the heathen, and punishments upon the people; to bind their kings with chains, and their nobles with fetters of iron; to execute upon them the judgment written: this honour have all his saints. Praise ye the Lord [Hallelujah!].*
> — PSALM 149:4-9

It's a habit of human behavior that we drift with whatever atmospheric season we are in. This is why we need to pause and pay attention to what is taking place in our lives. Where is God in our activities?

THROUGH EVERY TRIAL

If the Lord has blessed your life, there ought to be

something in your walk and talk that testifies of His goodness. Scripture says, *"Let the redeemed of the Lord say so"* (Psalm 107:2).

Psalm 149 gives us this opportunity. Here, David includes several snapshots of the victories of God's people over their enemies. While not specifically writing of the exodus from Egypt, crossing the Red Sea, and forty years wandering in the wilderness, we know what he is talking about—"binding kings and executing judgment."

He was praising God for all of Israel's victories.

Today, we can use the same words to thank the Lord for every trial He has brought us through and each triumph we have achieved.

A THREE-DIMENSIONAL PLAN

The major theme of Psalm 149 is abundance. First, abundance of joy to all the people of God (verses 1-5), then abundance of terror to their enemies (verses 6-9).

Attached to this psalm is a three-dimensional plan:

1. A Call to Praise (Psalm 149:1-3).

After exclaiming, "Praise the Lord," David calls

Israel to do exactly that, asking them to, *"Sing unto the Lord a new song"* (verse 1). This encouragement is nothing new. We find the same advice in Psalm 33:3; 40:3; 96:1; 98:1; and 144:9.

We are told in Psalm 95:1-3, *"O come, let us sing unto the Lord: let us make a joyful noise to the rock of our salvation. Let us come before his presence with thanksgiving, and make a joyful noise unto him with psalms. For the Lord is a great God, and a great King above all gods."*

In addition to singing, we are to praise God with musical instruments and dance: *"Praise him with the sound of the trumpet: praise him with the psaltery and harp. Praise him with the timbrel and dance: praise him with stringed instruments and organs. Praise him upon the loud cymbals: praise him upon the high sounding cymbals"* (Psalm 150:3-5).

What does this say to you and me? Look around. Find something—*anything*—and use it to exalt and praise the Lord.

- If you have nothing but keys in your pocket take them out, jingle them together and praise God with your keys!
- If you have a few coins in your hand, find a way to let them make a sound to the King.

- If you can't do anything but stomp you feet, go ahead! Make a loud, joyful noise and praise the Lord.

Use what you have to let the earth know you are excited that God Almighty is in your life.

2. A Cause for Praise (Psalm 149:4-5).

The next two verses give us the reason we should tell God how much we love and adore Him. "Why? *"For the Lord taketh pleasure in his people"* (verse 4). And for His gift of salvation, we are to *"be joyful"*—even singing while we are in our *"beds"* resting (verse 5).

Day and night you have countless reasons to lift Him up and thank Him for taking you through, helping you over, and bringing you out of trials and tribulations.

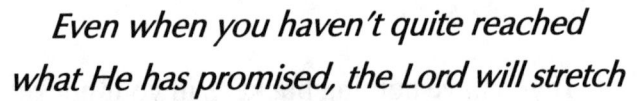

———————•»———————

Even when you haven't quite reached what He has promised, the Lord will stretch out His hand and give His favor to you.

You never have to look far to justify glorifying and magnifying His holy Name. Just the fact that your eyes opened this morning is worth a "Praise You, Lord."

3. To Conquer and Praise (Psalm 149:6-9).

The third part of this three-dimensional plan is to claim the territory and worship the One who made it all possible. David called on Israel to let the praises of God be in their mouth even as they had a *"sword in their hand"* (verse 6) to execute God's justice on the wicked (verses 7-8).

Even among their own people, Israel was being encouraged to put down evil antagonism against the Lord and His anointed.

There are elements in our own lives that will not leave by themselves—areas we need to take the sword to, cut out, and separate ourselves from. It is part of finding our liberty and being set free from the world.

At the same time, however, we can exclaim with the psalmist, "Praise ye the Lord" (verse 9).

"Hallelujah!" is your sound of release and relief. You need to shout it:

- Every time a bill gets paid.
- Every time a pain leaves your body.
- Every time a horrible situation changes.

- Every time you receive God's goodness.
- Every time you see the Master's handiwork.

Instead of finding a reason to be depressed, look up to heaven and shout "Hallelujah!"

Add Faith and Expectation

If you are tired of being where you are and have aspirations for the future, I have good news for you. There are unlimited possibilities ahead.

Take time to have a talk with Jesus and make sure that all is well with your soul. When things are right on the inside, no matter what the enemy does in his attempt to derail your destiny, you can tell him, "God's not finished with me yet!"

The words of Jesus still ring true: *"All things are possible to him who believes"* (Mark 9:23 NJKJV).

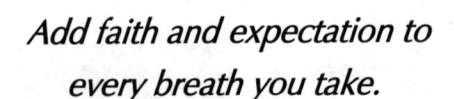

---

*Add faith and expectation to
every breath you take.*

Constantly claim God's promises and your status as a born again child of the King. In doing so, you will make the best of each moment and your hours will not be wasted.

The Lord has a vision for you and a timetable He expects you to keep, so take advantage of every minute. Don't be caught slacking off and avoiding your spiritual responsibilities.

If we are serious about the things of God, it's time for us to stop playing church. We need to get back to basics and ask the Lord to forgive us for wasting His time—and ours.

THE NORM, NOT THE EXCEPTION

Prayer, praise, and dance. These three acts of worship should surround our experience with the Lord. They shouldn't be just secret activities we do when no one is watching, but an inclusive part of ordinary worship! When the congregation gathers together, it should be the norm, not the exception, to lift our hands, raise our voices, and physically move our bodies in praise to the Lord.

This means everyone in the church. We all should be doing it together.

I believe in the Art of Worship. By this terminology I mean there should be a quality in the production and expression of how we personally praise and worship the Lord.

God has given us unique and separate personalities and some of us are more reserved than others. But in our own individual way we need to show the Lord how grateful and excited we are that He has saved our souls, healed our bodies, and delivered us from the clutches of Satan. Now this is worth shouting about!

If unbelievers are in your presence, they should learn something from you about our great God by the way they see you worship. It should make a permanent impact on their lives.

Your Christian Diet

Prayer, praise, and dance ministries are not supplements to your Christian diet, but are actual spiritual meals you receive before the main course of the spoken Word.

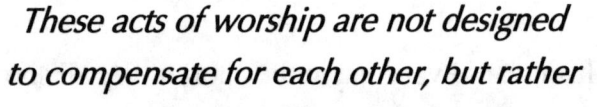

These acts of worship are not designed to compensate for each other, but rather to complement each other.

Prayer, praise, dance, and preaching are dynamic

moments of the worship service. Each one has the power to change lives. However, they are powerless if they don't give the Body of Christ access, provide order in worship, and alignment with His church.

As such, they should impart freshness, provoke change, awaken the hearer, connect heaven and earth, and testify of Jesus.

Each has its own distinct taste and carries its own divine fragrance. The expression can be of private interpretation, but each act is meant to become public property.

Never Serve it "Cold"

Prayer, praise, and dance should be regular parts of a church service. And because they are courses in your Christian diet they should never be "picked over" or served cold. Let me explain:

- **Cold Prayer**—uninviting, uninspired, seeks public approval, lacks prophecy, and is full of imbalanced rhetoric.

- **Cold Praise**—lacks enthusiasm (is not full of God), done out of obligation more than out of relationship with the Lord. It seems inconvenient.

- **Cold Dance**—doesn't flow. It is movement without a message, irreverent, lacks joy, a powerless presentation.

Examine your own life. Perhaps you can look back and see the rut you were once trapped in. Then you began to pray for God to make a way out of no way. Next, you decided to praise Him even though the answer had not yet appeared. Finally, at the end of your praise time, the Lord released a dance and you were moving in victory!

Divinely Inspired Words

Please realize that prayer itself is filled with prophecy. Your very words become activated by God Himself. If you feel the Lord moving in a certain direction, put it into words and let God take over from there.

Remember that prophecy is a divinely inspired foretelling, an utterance of God specifically released to reveal a message from the Father. It is for a particular purpose, place, and time.

This gift comes out of innocence and purity of thought. It is faith driven and spiritually motivated. Prophecy is not socially, emotionally, personality, or economically driven. It is *spiritually* driven.

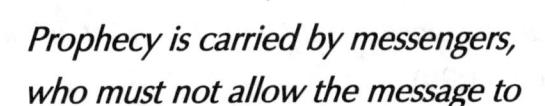

Prophecy is carried by messengers, who must not allow the message to be tarnished by carnality!

As a believer, you have the Word of God in your mouth; you just need to speak it out loud!

The church should be known by the world as not only a house of prayer and evangelism, but also as the place where God speaks to His children. We should be known as a prophetic people!

Have you asked the Lord to allow you to speak His Word in the earth? I believe He has given each of us a spirit of encouragement inside that is waiting to be released. Say what God inspires you to say.

"Give it Out!"

Prayer manages the emotion of the spirit. It also brings order to the demonstration of the spiritual gifts.

Our first obligation regarding prophecy is to listen, because it is heaven's turn to speak. Then we are to verbally speak it, because it's man's time to hear!

I believe this manifestation of the Spirit is for every believer who prays. As Moses told the children of Israel, *"Would God that all the Lord's people were prophets, and that the Lord would put his spirit upon them"* (Numbers 11:29).

The Apostle Paul writes, *"Follow after charity, and desire spiritual gifts, but rather that ye may prophesy"* (1 Corinthians 14:1). *"For he that prophesieth speaketh unto men to edification, and exhortation, and comfort"* (verse 3).

———————⟫———————

Without question, God has placed prophecy within you, but you must decide to give it out!

The Journey of the Ark

The reason David spoke so much on the topic of praise is because he remembered how the Lord had provided restoration in his own life.

After David became King of Israel and defeated the Philistines, there was one important matter to be dealt with. The Ark of the Covenant needed to be recovered and brought to Jerusalem. So he gathered his troops and headed for the house of Abinadab, where the Ark was hidden. Scripture records how *"they set the ark of God on a new cart, and brought it out of the house of Abinadab, which was on the hill...accompanying the ark of God...Then David and all the house of Israel played music before the Lord on all kinds of instruments of fir wood, on harps, on stringed instruments, on tambourines, on sistrums, and on cymbals"* (2 Samuel 6:4-5 NKJV).

DANCING IN THE STREETS

One of the rules God laid down was that no man was to physically touch the Ark itself. But on the journey, one of the oxen stumbled and a man named Uzzah reached out to steady the Ark. God's anger was unleashed and Uzzah died on the spot. So David had the Ark taken off the road and placed in the house of Obed-Edom—who became greatly blessed.

Three months later, David knew the Lord was pleased with his decision and decided to continue bringing the Ark to Jerusalem. It was an amazing procession!

Scripture tells us:

> *And so it was, when those bearing the ark of the Lord had gone six paces, that he sacrificed oxen and fatted sheep. Then David danced before the Lord with all his might; and David was wearing a linen ephod. So David and all the house of Israel brought up the ark of the Lord with shouting and with the sound of the trumpet.*
> *Now as the ark of the Lord came into the City of David, Michal, Saul's daughter, looked through a window and saw King David leaping and whirling before the Lord"* (2 Samuel 6:13-16 NKJV).

What a sight that must have been! The Ark of the Covenant was set in its place in the midst of the Tabernacle, and there David gave an offering of sacrifice to the Lord (verse 17). God was glorified.

Is it Really Necessary?

Today, our praise is not a single act but a perpetual demonstration of a lifestyle that promotes Jesus as our

Lord. And if you are praying and praising, dancing is sure to follow. In the house of the Lord it should be done with reverence, yet with joy and delight.

More than once I've been asked, "Why dance? Is that really necessary?"

In New Testament times, dancing was such a common part of daily life that it entered into children's games and activities. They imitated adults at religious events such as homecomings, weddings, and funerals.

Look at the story of the Prodigal Son. When he returned home after dabbling in the world of sin, his father ran out to meet him and said to his servants, *"'Bring the fatted calf here and kill it, and let us eat and be merry; for this my son was dead and is alive again; he was lost and is found.' And they began to be merry. Now his older son was in the field. And as he came and drew near to the house, he heard music and dancing"* (Luke 15:23-25 NKJV).

THAT'S DANCING!

When children would dance there were always those who, for whatever reason, would not participate. They were stubborn and proud, determined not to be pleased nor experience the pleasure of enacting and activating

God's liberty. This was the context of the remarks of Jesus when he said, speaking of the Pharisees, *"To what then shall I liken the men of this generation, and what are they like? They are like children sitting in the marketplace and calling to one another, saying: 'We played the flute for you, and you did not dance; we mourned to you, and you did not weep'"* (Luke 7:31 NKJV).

The flute symbolizes God's voice in the wind!
Have you heard Him speaking to you lately?
When are you going to dance?

I smile when people tell me, "Well I don't dance." I beg to differ with you.

- If you have ever bobbed you head with the beat—that's dancing!
- If you have ever rocked in a chair—that's dancing!
- If you have ever patted your feet—that's dancing!
- If you have ever moved your shoulders to the music—that's dancing!

- If you ever waved your arms—that's dancing!

Go Ahead and Dance!

Who is biblical dancing for? It's for men, women, and children who thank God for their salvation, see something great on the horizon and are willing to risk everything for the Lord.

When should you dance? At every turning point in your spiritual walk. At every new beginning.

You know how to pray. You know how to praise. Now go ahead and dance!

8

"I'm Going to Live Intentionally"

> *Truly God is good to Israel, even to such as are of a clean heart. But as for me, my feet were almost gone; my steps had well nigh slipped. For I was envious at the foolish, when I saw the prosperity of the wicked.*
>
> – Psalm 73:1-3

The psalmist had a problem. He looked around and saw people who weren't serving God attaining riches. He thought to himself, "How can it be that some who oppose the Lord live better than those who trust Him?"

Later in the chapter, we learn how he finds the answer to this dilemma. Yet there are millions of Christians today who are still asking the same question.

Believer or unbeliever, we have never been promised perpetual sunshine. Neither are we exempt from dark days and personal crisis. As Jesus tells us, *"He maketh his sun to rise on the evil and on the good, and sendeth rain on the just and on the unjust"* (Matthew 5:45).

I believe much of what we go through is because God is wanting us to understand who He is and what He has planned for our life.

DECISIONS, DECISIONS

By far, the most significant factor regarding how you live is how you handle your choices.

Look at your life today. The greatest part of who you are and what you are experiencing is the direct result of decisions you have made along the way. They can result in suffering or success.

We get upset when things are going downhill, yet in our frustration we choose options that make life even worse. On the other hand, when circumstances start improving, many just sit back and relax—thinking life will always be this easy. Suddenly, because of their laziness and not being serious about the future, their temporary success vanishes like a vapor.

This is why we need to treat every turning point with prayerful analysis and the attention it deserves. What are the pros? What are the cons? How will it affect my future?

To put it in a nutshell, you have got to live intentionally.

The reason I am a minister of the Gospel is because I believe that when a person's heart is right on the inside they will know how to deal with challenges on the outside. Repentance and salvation gives a clear purpose and focus to life.

God didn't place you on this planet to be miserable—even though you may go through unfortunate times. Your heavenly Father sent His Son to earth so you could have peace and hope as you journey through a sinful world.

Regardless of the circumstances, you always have something to thank God for. Let your appreciation show to Him and others!

What Truly Counts

Please understand that you are a constant, perpetual evangelist. You are either losing or wining a soul for Christ each time you enter into a conversation with a man, woman, or young person. I pray they can see the radiance of a loving God shining on your countenance.

What I am telling you has nothing to do with your present situation—how much money you owe, who gets on your nerves, how your friends treat you, or what is happening in your career. If the Lord dwells in your heart, that's all that counts

If your friend owns a five bedroom house and you only have a one room rental, relax. Don't get ulcers over it. I remember when I lived in a little studio apartment with a bed that converted into a couch during the daytime. There was one small table, a sparse kitchen, and a closet- size bathroom.

None of this mattered because at that point in my life I knew where I was headed—I was living intentionally.

I chose not to live beyond my means, and as result the day came when I saved enough to buy my own home.

My definition of living well is a roof over your head, clothes on your back, food to eat, a safe place to be—and the ability to take care of it all without being in a crisis. Everything over and above is the abundance and favor of God.

When you live intentionally, you will be comfortable and content where you are instead of being nervous of how you are going to pay the bills next month.

The Envy Factor

There is no need to be jealous of those whose lot in life seems to be far better than yours. If you aren't careful, you will be speaking like the psalmist:

> *For I was envious at the foolish, when I saw the prosperity of the wicked. For there are no bands in their death: but their strength is firm. They are not in trouble as other men; neither are they plagued like other men.*
>
> *Therefore pride compasseth them about as a chain; violence covereth them as a garment. Their eyes stand out with fatness: they have more than heart could wish.*
>
> *They are corrupt, and speak wickedly concerning oppression: they speak loftily. They set their mouth against the heavens, and their tongue walketh through the earth.*
>
> *Therefore his people return hither: and waters of a full cup are wrung out to them. And they say, How doth God know? and is there knowledge in the most High?* (Psalm 73:3-11).

Friend, don't let the prosperity of the wicked overwhelm you. Disappointment in life is meant to bring enlightenment, not depression.

Take Stock

When nothing seems to be working in your favor, it's time to take stock and evaluate the situation:

- Evaluation is meant to cause reckoning,
- Reckoning is meant to cause measuring,
- Measuring is meant to promote assessment,
- Assessment is meant to reveal corrective possibility and potential.
- Corrected potential should ultimately produce results.

What Was the Answer?

There may be occasions when God will block what you are doing to draw your attention back to Him. He knows what you need.

It took the psalmist a long time to get grievance out of his system. He continues, wallowing in his grief: *"Behold, these are the ungodly, who prosper in the world; they increase in riches. Verily I have cleansed my heart in vain, and washed my hands in innocency. For all the day long have I been plagued, and chastened every morning. If I say, I will speak thus; behold, I should offend against the generation of thy children"* (Psalm 73:12-15).

Finally, the answer came. The difference between the righteous and the wicked had nothing at all to do with money, it was all about their destiny!

What a revelation it was when God finally revealed that how we live determines *where* we will live. Our time on earth is all about preparing for eternity.

HE WENT TO THE SANCTUARY

Turn your attention to the revealing conclusion to this wisdom-filled psalm:

> *When I thought to know this, it was too painful for me; until I went into the sanctuary of God; then understood I their end. Surely thou didst set them in slippery places: thou castedst them down into destruction.*
>
> *How are they brought into desolation, as in a moment! they are utterly consumed with terrors. As a dream when one awaketh; so, O Lord, when thou awakest, thou shalt despise their image.*
>
> *Thus my heart was grieved, and I was pricked*

in my reins. So foolish was I, and ignorant: I was as a beast before thee. Nevertheless I am continually with thee: thou hast holden me by my right hand.

Thou shalt guide me with thy counsel, and afterward receive me to glory. Whom have I in heaven but thee? and there is none upon earth that I desire beside thee. My flesh and my heart faileth: but God is the strength of my heart, and my portion for ever.

For, lo, they that are far from thee shall perish: thou hast destroyed all them that go a whoring from thee. But it is good for me to draw near to God: I have put my trust in the Lord GOD, that I may declare all thy works. (Psalm 73:16-28).

Prosperity was not the issue. The psalmist said that when he went to the house of God, the answer was finally revealed. The Lord wasn't concerned with their wealth. The psalmist came to the conclusion that while the wicked may accumulate riches on this earth, it is only temporary. He was now receiving divine direction from God—and what the Lord gives no man can take away.

It is true. *"They that are far from thee shall perish"* (verse 27).

He realized that he was wasting his time trying to compare his life to someone else.

Don't Miss Your Blessing

How foolish to be selfish and greedy—spending God-given time being envious of others. Why should we care how another person seems to be blessed when we need the Lord to help us in our present situation?

If we continue to pay attention to the fortunes of others, we are likely to miss our blessing.

This is why the psalmist made the decision to live intentionally and seek only the promises of God.

Jesus gives us the same message when He says, *"But seek ye first the kingdom of God and his righteousness; and all these things shall be added unto you"* (Matthew 6:33).

I know that just as the Creator has made each of us unique individuals, He has something exclusively for you that no one else has or is experiencing. Please don't let your attention be diverted from His plan.

"My Portion Forever"

Long term blessings belong to men and women who are holy and righteous. And true holiness is born out of relationship with God, not the religious acts of men. It is revealed by intimately experiencing the Almighty, not being preoccupied with the world's traditions.

Holiness and righteousness aren't intended to cause bondage, but to enforce divine liberty. This is why truly sanctified believers are the freest people in the world!

Don't waste another minute. Start fulfilling what the Lord has assigned to your life. Recognize where your help is coming from. As the psalmist exclaims, *"My flesh and my heart fail; but God is the strength of my heart and my portion forever"* (Psalm 73:26 NKJV).

A Lifetime Commitment

The proof that you are living with purpose is that you are thanking God for all things. Your time on earth must be centered around Him.

As I have said before, if you are not living intentionally, you are probably living accidentally. This means you are more *reactive* than *proactive*.

It is my prayer that you will put what you have

learned into practice. Let me encourage you to tell the Lord:

- "Something marvelous is happening in me!"
- "I am seeking God's purpose, power, and passion."
- "I have decided to join the "Happy People."
- "I know that I am improved, impressive, and magnificently designed."
- "I will celebrate God's greatness and pass it on!"
- "I will reach new spiritual heights."
- "I will give the Lord unlimited praise."
- "I am going to live intentionally!"

By making a commitment to live by these principles you will be able to shout from your soul the final words of the book of Psalms, *"Praise the Lord!"*

INTENTIONAL LIVING

NOTES

FOR ADDITIONAL RESOURCES
OR TO SCHEDULE THE AUTHOR FOR
SPEAKING ENGAGEMENTS, CONTACT:

BISHOP SIMON GORDON
TRIEDSTONE CHURCH
1415 WEST 104TH STREET
CHICAGO, IL 60643

PHONE: 773-881-7710
INTERNET: www.triedstonefgbc.com